Watchmen On the Walls

Watchmen On the Walls

**Pastors Equipping Christians
For Their Civil Duties**

Bruce Anderson
Mark Beliles
Stephen McDowell

Providence
Foundation

Charlottesville, Virginia

Watchmen on the Walls:
Pastors Equipping Christians for their Civil Duties

First Printing, 1995

Published by:
The Providence Foundation
P.O. Box 6759
Charlottesville, VA 22906
(804) 978-4535

Cover design:
Jeremiah Pent
Graphicom
P.O. Box 10720
Ft. Worth, TX 76114
(817) 625-5500

The Providence Foundation is a Christian educational organization whose purpose is to assist in the development of liberty, justice, and prosperity among the nations by teaching and equipping people in a Biblical philosophy of life. The Foundation teaches Christian principles of government and politics, economics and business, arts and sciences, education and family life, using historical models which illustrate their application.

Printed in the United States of America

ISBN 1-887456-02-3

Watchmen on the Walls

Table of Contents

Introduction

Watchmen on the Walls is written for the purpose of:
1. Showing Christians they have God-given duties that extend to the civil realm.
2. Teaching biblical principles of public life.
3. Communicating to pastors their responsibility to equip Christians in their civil duties.
4. Giving pastors suggestions of how to prepare their church members to be salt in the public arena.

This book is especially addressed to pastors for, as teachers and leaders in the church, they play a vital role in reforming our nation. The church shapes the character and thinking of the people who in turn shape the character and direction of the nation. As De Tocqueville observed 150 years ago, the source of America's greatness and liberty lies in the churches of America – not just any churches, though, but those whose pulpits are aflame with righteousness and whose message encompasses all of life.

In regard to the public life of the nation, ministers should be "watchmen on the walls" educating the people in biblical principles as applied to all of life, so that the people will know the right views to hold and the proper action to take when danger threatens them and their nation. A knowledgeable citizenry is essential for liberty and to obtain this we need a knowledgeable clergy. All may then recognize the enemy, sound the alarm, and protect our God-given unalienable rights.

Watchmen on the Walls

PASTORS EQUIPPING CHRISTIANS FOR THEIR CIVIL DUTIES

"I have posted watchmen on your walls, O Jerusalem; they will never be silent day or night..." (Is. 62:7).

"...They keep watch over you as men who must give an account" (Heb. 13:7).

"...Stand in the courtyard of the Lord's house and speak to all the people of the towns of Judah who come to worship in the house of the Lord. Tell them everything I command you; do not omit a word" (Jer. 26:2).

"For I have not hesitated to proclaim to you the whole will of God" (Acts 20:27).

"You are the salt of the earth.... You are the light of the world" (Mt. 5:13, 14).

"To many of the clergy the spirit of the day seemed disorderly and lawless and they feared for the welfare of the government. They believed it their peculiar business to be 'watchmen on the tower', to scent out and warn against danger and to set men right as to the principles upon which they were to act and the views they were to hold."

— Historian Alice M. Baldwin of the New England Clergy at the time of the American Revolution.

Chapter 1

What Americans Think of the Church Today

Research by notable pollster, George Barna, "underscores the unflattering image of the local church that many people possess."[1] **Overall, just 28% of all Americans strongly agree "that the Christian churches in their area are relevant to the way they live today."[2]**

Barna observes that American society is crumbling at many points — economically, politically, educationally, and morally. But, "the indications are that Christians are not sufficiently armed for the struggle."[3] According to Barna, here are some signs of the church's inability to deal with the social, cultural, and political issues of today:[4]

- The spiritual walk of Christian individuals has been retarded by their frequent, if unconscious, support of philosophies and activities contradictory to the Christian perspective.

- Despite millions of dollars spent on media ministry and evangelistic publishing, there has been no real growth in the size of the Christian population in the past five years.

- By and large Christians are politically illiterate. Despite heightened awareness in some issue areas, the majority of Christians remain inactive and unconcerned about policy developments.

Barna's study of pastors from healthy, growing churches demonstrated that "relevance was a key word" in their ministries. "They were emphatic that the gospel is relevant to the very struggles and issues that fill the evening news and which throb in the minds of Americans....[They] were passionate in describing how the gospel can be made the blueprint to meaningful response" in the world.[5]

Popular Christian scholar and author, Os Guinness, once said, "Recently a historian commented on what he had observed of the Christian faith in America: 'Socially irrelevant, even if privately engaging.' "[6]

These observations of Barna and Guinness are challenging to us as pastors! **Do you feel that you and your church have been as relevant as you should be to the needs of your community?** What follows is intended to help you think through the role of pastors and the church with respect to their relevance to society.

We would first ask, **"What are pastor's doing?"**

Chapter 2

Are Pastors Teaching on Civil Duties?

We have noted that the church is considered irrelevant. This would seem to imply that the work of pastors — those who are leading the church — is also irrelevant. Are we pastors irrelevant because we are not addressing the real issues and needs of daily American life in the 1990's?

Think of the sermons you've preached or heard over the last few years. What topics or books of the Bible were covered? Were there any messages on the Ten Commandments? Were there any on the Christian's duty to the poor? Or were there any on government? Has there been any coverage of Leviticus or Deuteronomy?

Here is a sermon analysis exercise to help you evaluate your use of the Bible in your ministry:

SERMON ANALYSIS

In the past three years, how many times did you teach or preach on the following Biblical topics:

1. Salvation   _____
2. Prayer   _____
3. Faith   _____
4. Holiness   _____
5. Sin   _____
6. The Church   _____
7. Family   _____
8. Civil Government   _____
9. The Ten Commandments   _____
10. Spiritual Growth   _____
11. The Great Commission   _____
12. Christian Civil Duties   _____
13. Christian Social Duties   _____
14. Education   _____
15. Economics or Finances   _____
16. The Book of Ephesians   _____
17. The Book of Deuteronomy   _____

The results of this sermon analysis can help us pinpoint some of those areas to which we need to give more attention in our ministries. Think also of the overall ministry of your church, its ministries, classes, and programs.

Most likely, in our preaching and in the overall ministry of the church, we are not giving enough attention to biblical teachings on government and society. The Bible deals with the subject of government twice as much as it does with personal matters. For example, consider the many books of the Bible that deal with the government of Israel.

Similarly, Jesus spent more time teaching about money than about prayer and faith combined. Jesus quoted the book of Deuteronomy more than any other book in the Bible. Furthermore, any of us would agree that the Ten Commandments are one of the most basic teachings of Christianity. As will be explained, government, economics, and law receive a great deal of attention in the Bible and Jesus' teaching. **But how much attention are they receiving in your pulpit and in the overall ministry of your church? — Is it enough?** Someone has suggested it would be a telling experiment if we could see what a typical pastor's Bible would look like today if it were based on what he preaches. Would it be skinny or include only select books, pages, or topics? If so, an examination of parishioners' lives would likely reflect this deficiency.

Next we ask: **"What should pastors be doing?"**

Chapter 3

Christians' Civil Duties and the Role of Pastors

The irrelevance of pastors may have to do with our ministry training and understanding of the Bible and Christian mission. Perhaps, too, our concerns about slipping into the "social gospel" and other misconceptions of the church's role in society are causing us to hold back. Let's rethink some basic presuppositions of Christianity — the role of the Bible and the nature of the Christian mission — and their implications for pastoral ministry and the mission of the church.

According to the Bible, what should the pastor be teaching?

The starting point for the Christian is the Bible, God's revealed will. The Bible is absolute truth. When we deny the total truth and authority of the Bible, something else takes its place — independent human reason, scientism, or pragmatism. To reject the authority of Scripture is to reject the Lordship of Christ. **Therefore, we should not base our understanding of pastoral ministry and the overall ministry of the church simply on tradition, "good ideas," or whatever seems to**

**work, but rather on exactly what the Bible tells us to do —
no more, no less.**

The Scriptures tell us what are the pastor's duties. We must
not assign a duty to pastors which is not assigned them in
Scripture. At the same time, we must not neglect or reject any
duty that **is** assigned pastors in Scripture. Pastors are obligated
by the authority of Scripture to fulfill **all** the duties it assigns
them, not just some of those duties.

What parts of the Bible should pastors teach? Scripture
makes this clear: *"All Scripture is God-breathed and is useful
for teaching, rebuking, correcting, and training in righteousness, so that the man of God may be thoroughly equipped for
every good work"* (2 Tim. 3:16,17, NIV). *"All Scripture"*
means the man of God must use **all** of the Bible and **all** of the
Bible's doctrines to teach, rebuke, correct, and train his flock.
By mining **all** parts of Scripture, the minister will be **thoroughly** equipped for **every** good work. **It is only by using all
of the Bible's teaching that we can fulfill our pastoral
duties.** Ministers often assume the primary pastoral duty is
converting people to Christ, but is it more than that?

> ## Does the Christian mission go beyond converting people to Christ?

Since the Bible is authoritative as to our duties, let's consider
what the Bible tells us about our mission. The Christian mission
is comprehensive in nature. God has revealed himself as both
the King of creation and the Redeemer of mankind. His
kingship over creation is depicted in the opening chapters of
the Bible; God created man in His own image and likeness as
His vice-regent or steward to rule over the earth. Unfortunately,

man fell from the purpose for which God created him — to rule and to cultivate the garden (Gen. 1:26-28; 2:15). Thus, man lost both his intimate relationship with God and his ability to properly govern the earth.

God's redemptive nature is also evident in the opening chapters of the Bible. Man having fallen from what God made him to be and to do, God planned both to redeem man and to restore man's delegated authority and stewardship over the earth. God promised that the seed of woman (referring to Jesus) would destroy the serpent (Satan; Gen. 3:15).

The story of redemption unfolds in the various covenants which God initiated with men. The giving of the law in the Mosaic Covenant was also used by God to further His redemptive program. Of course, God's redemptive purpose has found ultimate fulfillment in the New Covenant through Christ, who was slain and by whose blood God has redeemed men for himself "from every tribe and tongue and people and nation" (Rev. 5:9).

We have been redeemed *for a purpose*. **In Christ, we have been restored to sonship and are now in a position to obey two great mandates God has given us — the Cultural Mandate and the Evangelistic Mandate.**

With respect to the cultural mandate, God has restored us to stewardship. Through Christ, we are called back to God's original purpose — to live in his image and to *"Be fruitful and increase in number; fill the earth and subdue it. Rule over... every living creature that moves on the ground"* (Gen. 1:28). We have been restored to serving God as his vice-regent over the earth. This Cultural Mandate, also referred to as the Creation Commission, calls us to use all our resources to express

His image and likeness on the earth. Fulfilling this mandate requires us to discover truth through the sciences, to apply truth through technology, to interpret truth through the humanities, to implement truth through commerce, and to transmit truth through education.[6]

With respect to the second of the two great mandates, God has also redeemed us for the ministry of reconciliation (2 Cor. 5:17-19; Lk. 24:47). This can be referred to as **the Evangelistic Mandate** or **Redemption Commission** and is known and emphasized by most pastors.

What some do not recognize, however, is that **the Great Commission** actually embraces **both** the Creation and Redemption Commissions:

"All authority in heaven and on earth has been given to me. Therefore go and make disciples of all nations, baptizing them in the name of the Father and of the Son and of the Holy Spirit, and teaching them to obey everything I have commanded you. And surely I will be with you always, to the very end of the age" (Mt. 28:18-20, NIV).

The comprehensive nature of the commission is clear. It calls us to lead not only individuals into the Lordship of Christ, but whole nations. Matthew Henry said that "the principal intention of this commission" is clear; it is to "do your utmost to make the nations Christian nations."

The Great Commission calls us not only to convert and baptize the nations, but to teach them to obey **"everything"** Christ commanded. **"Everything"** includes obedience not only to those commands related to salvation, prayer, Bible reading, and ministering to others but to "all" that Christ has taught us — including His teaching about family relationships, civil government, money management, and so on. The Great Commission is truly great!

We must ask ourselves whether or not we as Christians today are faithful to **both** commissions. Often, we focus only on the Redemption Commission, neglecting the Creation Commission. We teach the Great Commission as only an evangelistic mandate that deals with conversion and a select set of spiritual disciplines. We neglect to teach it as a mandate calling for the conversion and comprehensive discipleship of nations. The Great Commission has the restoration of all things in view, including society and government (Col. 1:15-20). Some American Christians are evangelistic, but are we discipling the nations of the world?

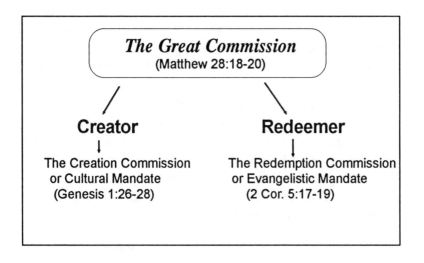

Does the Bible teach us about society and government?

The Bible is full of teachings regarding social affairs and civil government. The charts on page 19 and 20 list some of these. Biblical teachings about the state (or civil government) must be viewed in relation to God's overall purpose for the state.

A fundamental principle taught in the Scriptures that should form the basis for our involvement in civil affairs is the idea that the state is of Divine origin and fulfills a specific purpose in God's plan in history. Many Christians today believe that God only ordained two institutions—the family and the church. Consequently, they are less likely to be involved in the state since it is of human origin. If they are involved in political and social activities it is with the view of winning the civil war of values to protect the family and church. While this is certainly important for us to do, what becomes of the Christians' involvement in civil government when the danger wanes? They will likely retreat from the civic arena until the next threat looms large enough to stir them to action. With such a view the battle will never be won. We must see, therefore, that just as God created the family and placed us in it to fulfill certain duties and responsibilities, He also created the state, placing us in it to fulfill its God ordained function.

The book of Genesis reveals how God founded the family, hence, rooting the believer in an unwavering commitment to his marriage and his children. The book of Genesis also reveals how God established the state, hence, it is of Divine origin, and believers should be just as committed to their obligations in this sphere of life.

Before man's rebellion against God in the Garden of Eden, there was no need for civil government to protect men from each other. However, when man fell he took on a sinful nature which destroyed his capacity for self-government. This led to Cain killing Abel and violence filling the earth (see Genesis 6).

After God brought Noah safely through the flood, He repeated the Cultural Mandate that had been given to Adam, but then added the responsibility for punishment of criminals in order to protect innocent human life in a fallen world. God said in Genesis 9:6 that if a man murdered another man, then mankind should put the murderer to death.

Here is the foundation of civil government as a Divine institution, created for the purpose of protecting the righteous, punishing criminals, and upholding justice. This basic purpose for government is affirmed in the New Testament in Romans 13 and 1 Peter 2.

Paul clearly upholds the idea that civil government is a Divine institution when he states that the civil magistrate is a "minister of God" and that there is no civil authority that God did not establish. Almost all of the Apostolic, Catholic, and Orthodox fathers of the faith, as well as most of the confessions of faith coming out of the Protestant Reformation, taught that the state is an institution of Divine origin and purpose.

If we view the state in this light, it will be natural for us to fulfill our governmental duties and responsibilities as taught in the Bible. One such duty of citizens is to "choose wise, understanding, and knowledgeable men...(to be) rulers over you" (Deuteronomy 1:13-15). According to Scripture every citizen is accountable for who governs him. Rulers are to be "knowledgeable" of God's higher law, but are also to be "able men, such as fear God, men of truth, hating covetousness" (Exodus 18:21). This means that political party affiliation or specific stands on issues are not as important as basic godliness and morality in leadership. These rulers were to "judge the people...in every small matter" or "case" (Exodus 18:22,26).

A New Testament reference to this Biblical duty of citizenship is found in 1 Corinthians 5 and 6, where Paul states that although not all individual Christians are responsible for exercising civil judgment directly, nonetheless, we **are** all responsible for selecting godly judges so that we do not end up having to settle civil disputes in courts run by pagan judges. Although the primary point in the 6th chapter of Corinthians is to avoid civil suits against other believers, the argument Paul makes begins with the premise in verse 2 that "the saints will judge the world." Certainly this will be true after Christ returns, but also applies, as Paul says in verse 3, to "much **more** the things of **this life.**"

In other words, Christians should be involved in learning how to govern **now** in preparation for the future. Paul asks also in verse 2: "If you are to judge the world, are you not competent to judge trivial cases?" This reference to "judging trivial cases" is a clear allusion to the passage in Exodus 18 when citizens were commanded by God to elect civil representatives to "judge the people...in every small case" (Ex.. 18:22,26).

The Bible requires more of us than simply praying for political leaders and paying our taxes. To elect godly candidates is a duty for which we will be accountable to God. In modern times the vehicle through which candidates for public office are nominated and placed on the ballot is called a "political party." If believers neglect involvement in the local political party of their choice then unbelievers will determine who will be on the ballot. This almost always leaves the Christian with the unhappy prospect of choosing in the general election among candidates who do **not** fulfill the Biblical criteria for public office. Therefore, the only way for Christians to be truly faithful to their Biblical duty of selecting Godly rulers is to be consistently attending the meetings of their local political party when the initial nominating takes place. Failure to do this will result in ungodly government officials making the laws under which we live.

Paul says in verse 5 of 1 Corinthians 6 that if Christians are not selecting godly rulers and end up taking their disputes to pagan-run courts, they should be ashamed. This was particularly true of these Corinthian believers who, living in Greece where there was a tradition of free elections of local rulers, their neglect of their Biblical duty as citizens was even more shameful.

When Paul came to Corinth, he brought a team of ministers, one of whom was a man named Erastus (Acts 19:22). Erastus would later become a government official in Corinth — "the Director of Public Works" or "City Treasurer" — as Paul noted in his letter to the Roman Christians (Rom. 16:23). Here is an example of a man "esteemed by the church," a minister of the Gospel, and extremely close to the Apostle Paul, who entered the political arena to be a godly ruler in "things of **this** life" (1 Cor. 6:4).

The New Testament has other examples of political action. Acts 16 records that Paul championed civil liberty by protesting the violation of his civil rights when he was arrested, beaten and thrown into jail without just cause. When Paul and Silas did not escape after an earthquake freed them from their chains and prison doors, the jailer and his family were converted. The next morning the city officials sent word to release the prisoners, but since there was no apology or acknowledgment that what had happened was a violation of his civil rights, Paul sent back word that he would not leave until the officials came themselves and corrected this wrong. The magistrates capitulated to Paul's demands, personally coming to appeal to him. Then, and only then, did the great apostle go on his way. If only the evangelistic mandate was important to Paul, the opportunity to get out of prison and continue his gospel ministry would have been seen as an answer to prayer, but Paul was committed to fulfilling both the evangelistic and cultural commissions of Christ. To protest civil tyranny was just as important to Paul as preaching salvation to the lost.

Social and Cultural Teachings of the Bible

- Marriage and divorce (Mt. 5:27-32; Lk. 16:18; 1 Cor. 7:1-10)
- Family relations (Eph. 5:22-33; Col. 3:18-20)
- Child rearing (Eph. 6:1-4; Col. 3:21)
- Duty to the poor (Mt. 25:31-46; Lk. 16:19-25; 2 Cor. 8:13ff)
- Employer-employee relationships (Eph. 6:5-9; Lk. 10:17)
- Honest wages (1 Tim. 5:18; Lk. 10:7)
- Free-market bargaining (Mt. 20:1-15)
- Private property rights (Acts 5:4)
- Godly citizenship and the proper function of the state (Rom. 13:1-7; 1 Pet. 2:13-17)
- The family as the primary agency of welfare (1 Tim. 5:8)
- Proper use of finances (Mt. 5:14ff)
- The dangers of debt (Rom. 13:8)
- The morality of investment (Mt. 25:14-30)
- The obligation to leaving an inheritance (2 Cor. 12:14)
- Penal restraints upon criminals (Rom. 13:4; 1 Tim. 1:8-10)
- Lawsuits (1 Cor. 6:1-8)
- And more[7]

Civil Teachings of the Bible

1. The state as a divine institution for the purpose of protecting law-abiding citizens and punishing criminals (Gen. 9:1, 6; Rom. 13:3, 4; 1 Pet. 2:13, 14)

2. Decentralization of civil power (federalism; Deut. 16:18, 19; 2 Chron. 19:5-10)

3. Written constitution (Ex. 20-23; Ex. 19:5-8; Ex. 20:2-17; 1 Chron. 11:3; Deut. 17:14-20).

4. Separation of powers (Is. 33:22; Ex. 4:29)

5. Independent judges and juries (2 Chron. 19:5-10; Ex. 23:1-3; Deut. 17:6; Deut. 19:15-19; Lev. 20)

6. Equality before the law (Ex. 12:49; Lev. 24:22; Num. 15:15, 16, 29)

7. Civilian militia and police forces (Deut. 20:9, 10; Num. 31:3, 14; 1 Sam. 25:13)

8. Bicameral legislature (Ex. 24:1; Num. 11:16, 17; Ex. 18:12, 21, 22)

9. Election of representatives (Deut. 1:13; Ex. 18:17-27)

10. Consent of the governed, the right to vote, and the right of representation (1 Chron. 28:1-8; 1 Chron. 29:22; 2 Chron. 23:11) [8]

Did Jesus teach us about society and government?

We know Christ told us we must teach the nations to obey *"everything I have commanded you."* **So what did Christ command? Has he charged us with a set of truths that are solely internal, personal, or mystical? No. The scope of His teaching is very broad.** If the church neglects the cultural impact of the gospel, many people will only see Christianity as a mere pietistic religion with no real relevance to life on earth.

Jesus taught more about public affairs than is commonly believed by many. There are many social and cultural teachings of Jesus recorded in the New Testament including, for example, marriage and divorce (Mt. 5:27-32), duty to the poor (Mt. 25:31-46), and the proper use of finances (Mt. 5:14ff). Jesus has also taught us principles of civil government (see the chart on page 22).[9]

The civil teachings of Jesus have transformed the world. For example, He taught that civil rulers are to be public servants (in Luke 22:25-26 and Matthew 20:25-26), hence, government exists to serve man. This idea has permeated most of the world and brought drastic changes in eliminating the top-down rule of the tyrant while increasing the bottom-up rule of the citizen. Governing officials in America today are called *public servants*. Many nations use the term *minister* or *prime minister* when speaking of their governing officials. *Minister* means *servant*. Where did the idea of calling civil leaders, *servants*, come from? It originated from the teaching of Jesus about 2000 years ago.

Civil Teachings of Jesus Christ

1. God created and is sovereign over civil government (John 19:11).

2. Government is due the taxes and services of its citizens (Mt. 17:24-27; Mt. 22:17-21).

3. Government jurisdiction is limited (Mt. 22:17-21).

4. Individuals have inherent value (Mt. 6:26; Mt. 9:12; Mt. 10:31; Mt. 22:17-21).

5. Mosaic law is applicable today (Mt. 5:17-38; Mt. 15:4; Mt. 19:7-19; Jn. 8:1-7).

6. Government is to serve all men equally (Lk. 22:25-26; Jn. 4:7-9; Mt. 20:25-26).

7. Social change is to be gradual and democratic, internal to external (Mt. 19:3-8; Mt. 28:19; Acts 1:6-8; Lk. 19:11-17).

8. Political and legal means can be used to achieve social justice (Lk. 19:11-17; Mt. 12:18-21; Lk. 18:2-8; Mt. 23:23).

9. Governmental injustice is to be resisted through protest, flight, and force in self-defense (Lk. 10:11; Mt. 10:17-23; Lk. 22:35-38; Mt. 26:51-52; Lk. 12:58; Mt. 27:14; Lk. 18:1-5; Lk. 10:10-11; Lk. 13:31-32; Mt. 3:1-4; Mk. 11:15-16).

10. Military strength can be used to maintain peace (Lk. 11:21-22; Lk. 14:31; Lk. 22:36-38).

In Matthew 22, Jesus made it clear that we all have duties toward government by commanding us to "render to Caesar the things that are Caesar's." In chapter 23 He rebuked the Pharisees for insisting on the ecclesiastical duty of tithing while "neglecting the weightier matters" such as "justice." (This same fault is evident in most churches in America today where tithing is part of basic discipleship and sermons, but civil duties are ignored.) Jesus also taught the ideas of limited government and resistance to tyranny in other passages.

To summarize, the teachings of Jesus and of the Bible are very broad, including a wide range of governmental and social topics. Previously, we discussed the duty of pastors to teach all the Bible. **The conclusion, then, is that pastors have the duty to teach the governmental and social teachings of the Bible.**

Shouldn't revival and prayer be our emphasis?

Some might say that all this talk about government is not that important because "all we need is a revival and awakening of Christianity." This **is** greatly needed because all change in a nation begins in the hearts of men. However, along with revival and awakening we need also to see a reformation of society. Revival and reformation represent aspects of the two commissions — Creation and Redemption — discussed previously. We are called to go beyond evangelism to comprehensive discipleship. This calling includes **both** revival **and** reformation.

The ingredients of revival—spiritual knowledge, intimacy with God, and true religion—are never separated from social and political justice in the Bible: *"He defended the cause of the poor and needy, and so all went well. Is that not what it means to know me? declares the Lord"* (Jer. 22:16). *"Religion that God our Father accepts as pure and faultless is this: to look after orphans and widows in their distress and to keep oneself from being polluted by the world" (James 1:27). "...And what does the Lord require of you? To act justly and to love mercy and to walk humbly with your God" (Mic. 6:8).*

The Bible gives us an example of a revival of religion accompanied by a reformation of society in the account of the rule of Josiah (2 Chron. 34-35). Early in his reign, after discovering the truth of God's law, he purified the temple and destroyed false idols, doing what was right in the eyes of the Lord. He also removed the evil in the city gates (public life) and throughout the land (2 Kings 23:8, 24-25). When they found the lost Book of the Law, Josiah wept and humbled himself because Israel had not kept all God's commands. He then committed all the people and the nation to the commandments of the Lord, thereby returning Israel to biblical standards of righteousness for society and bringing about reform.

Nehemiah was one who not only fasted and prayed for his nation (Neh. 1:4), but also took action. Along with his prayers, he initiated discussion with King Artaxerxes (a pagan king) on behalf of the Israelites (Neh. 2:5). He found favor with the king and acquired his permission, protection, and financial support for the purpose of rebuilding Jerusalem (Neh. 2:5-9). Nehemiah successfully went on to lead the Israelites as governor and brought about reforms based on God's law.

While it is clearly the duty of every Christian to pray for political leaders (1 Tim. 2:1-2), we have seen that it is not our **only** political duty. Christ commanded us to "give to Caesar what is Caesar's." This means that we have obligations toward government in the eyes of God that are not optional. A number of our duties in civil affairs have already been mentioned; others will be mentioned.

Isn't the church supposed to be separate from the family and the state?

So the Bible teaches us about government and society. "But isn't there a separation of church and state?" Yes, but not a separation of God and government. Since, as Jesus taught (in John 19:11), God created and is sovereign over civil government, it would be hard to separate God from government. While many governments do not acknowledge God, they, nonetheless, have their foundation in religion or the faith of the people. The predominant faith or world view held by the citizens dictates a basic morality which will be reflected by those who govern the nation and make the laws. So all governments, and laws that flow from them, are built upon some religion or world view which provides the basis for right and wrong behavior in society. Therefore, the source of the law of a society is the god of that society. If the Bible is the source of law, of what is right and wrong behavior and action, then the God of the Bible is the god of that society; if man is the source of law, where a majority or ruling minority determines what is right and wrong, then man is the god of that society (this is secular humanism).

The source of law and morality in America has been the Christian religion. Accepted universal societal behavior such as not stealing, not committing murder, and honest dealings with others came from the Bible. We do not want to separate such biblical principles from government.

We, also, do not want to separate the church from teaching such principles. The pastor and church have the duty to teach Christians everything Christ commanded them, including those teachings that relate to the family and the state. The church has authority to speak the truth to all institutions in society — the church is "the pillar and foundation of the truth" (1 Tim. 3:15). In terms of speaking the truth, it must not be separate from the family or the state. The church must inform them, for **the church builds the people, and the people build the nation.**

Therefore, one part of the pastor's ministry is to build up the people so they will be equipped to build up the nation. This is one aspect of the overall duty of pastors which is *"to prepare God's people for works of service"* (Eph. 4:12). "Works of service" is a broad term. To what does it refer? The pastor's duty *"to prepare God's people for works of service"* **refers to the comprehensive nature of the Christian mission.** As previously discussed, the Christian mission is related to God Himself and to His mission, and His mandates for men.

Though God and government are not to be separated, the Bible does distinguish several different institutions in society, each having a unique sphere of authority or jurisdiction delegated by God. These institutions are to be separate from one another with none in authority over any other, but all under the authority of God. The biblical conception of society may be diagrammed as follows:

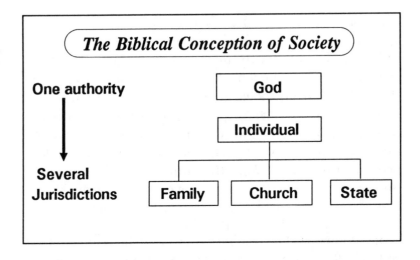

Within the Christian mission, the responsibilities of the church are to be distinguished from that of the family and the state. This conception of jurisdictional sovereignty of distinct institutions in society was established by Jesus Christ in one of His most significant civil teachings. Matthew 22:17-21 records how Jesus used a coin with Caesar's image upon it to illustrate that civil government does indeed have certain jurisdictional authority, such as in the area of taxation. However, Christ went on to pronounce that the state's jurisdiction is limited when He said that we are to render "to God the things that are God's." The inference is that there is a sphere of life where civil government (i.e. Caesar) has no jurisdiction at all. That sphere was defined here as involving the soul and mind of men, being made, not in Caesar's image, but in the image of God. Jesus was affirming that religious worship and opinions, and any endeavor relating to thoughts or speech, must remain completely free from government control.

Thomas Jefferson reiterated this truth when he wrote in his

Virginia Statute for Religious Freedom that "God hath created the mind free." The principles of separation of church and state, and, separation of schools, press and speech from the control of the state, which are articulated in the First Amendment of the Constitution, are rooted in this historic political teaching of Christ. Before Christianity, the pagan world always included religion and education under the jurisdiction of the state. It was a radical political concept for Christ to declare that Caesar's power should be limited and, therefore, was used against Jesus when He was convicted of treason and crucified under Roman law. Christ's teaching has since changed the western world.

What then are the purposes and responsibilities of the individual and the three Divine institutions? According to the Bible, the duties assigned to the individual, the family, the church, and the state are as follows:[10]

The Individual's Purpose and Responsibilities:

1. **Worship** —*"Love the Lord your God..."* (Lk. 10:27; Deut. 6:5)

   * *Man's primary purpose is to glorify God and enjoy him forever.*
   a. Personal prayer, Bible reading/study/meditation
   b. Assemble with other believers
   c. Sabbath observance

2. **Charity** — *"...Love your neighbor.."* (Lk. 10:27; Lev. 19:9-18; Mt. 25:35-36)

   * *The Golden rule: Do unto others as you would have them do unto you.*
   a. Assist the needy and show mercy

b. Speak the truth—evangelism, exhortation, edification
c. Involvement in society/government (conversion of institutions)

3. Work —*"...as [you love] yourself"* (Lk. 10:27; Gen. 1:26-28; Gen. 2:15)

* *That man is God's creation and made in God's image is the foundation for self-worth, self-preservation, human dignity, and work.*
a. Provide for self and family — individuals will start businesses and create wealth
b. Bless the nations — occurs as individuals provide needed goods and services

The Family's Purpose and Responsibilities:

1. Procreation (Gen. 1:28; 1 Tim. 5:10, 14)

* *Be fruitful and multiply.*
a. Pro-life — sanctity of life (Gen. 9:6)
b. Children — a blessing (Ps. 127:3-5)

2. Education (Deut. 6:6-7)

* *"You shall teach your sons."*
a. Fit children to fulfill their individual purposes and responsibilities (Prov. 22:6)
b. Build godly character (Gen. 18:19)
c. Train in a biblical world view (Ps. 78:5)
d. Discipline as well as instruction (Eph. 6:4)

3. Health and Welfare

* *Practice hospitality, especially for those of your own household.*
a. Preventative health care — proper exercise, nutri-

tion, sanitation
b. Taking care of the sick, elderly, orphan, widow
(1Tim. 5:4,8,10,16; Deut. 15:7,8,11; Deut. 14:28-29)
c. Saving and investing for your retirement and your
posterity (2 Cor. 12:14; Prov. 19:14; Deut. 21:17)

The Church's Purpose and Responsibilities:

**1. Regular instruction of members in biblical truth for
every sphere of life**

a. Sunday preaching, regular classes, and other educational means (Mt. 28:18-20; 2 Tim. 3:16-17)
b. Includes starting schools and colleges

2. Administer sacraments and church discipline (1 Cor.
5:8-13; 1 Cor. 11:23-25; Mt. 18:15-17)

a. Corporate worship and sacrifice (Gen. 4:3-5, 26)
b. Baptism and Lord's Supper
c. Excommunication

3. Discipling, equipping, and organizing believers (Eph.
4:11-12, 16; Titus 3:8, 14)

a. Providing coordination and support for individuals
and families to work in voluntary union with others
to fulfill their purpose
b. Pastors are to be role models of what the church
teaches in their personal conduct and through their
involvement in society.

The Civil Government's (State's) Purpose and Responsibilities:

1. Protect the righteous, i.e. law-abiding citizens (Rom. 13:3-4; 1 Pet. 2:13-14)

a. Protection of life (Ex. 20:13), liberty (Ex. 21:6), and property (Ex. 20:15) from domestic and foreign law-breakers. (Governments are to secure God-given inalienable rights.)

b. Government coordinates civilian police for order and army for defense.

c. Protection of rights from government abuse (via decentralized government, separation of powers, election of representatives)

2. Punish the evil doer, i.e. criminal (Ex. 20:13; Ex. 21:12; Ex. 22:2)

a. Set up constitution with just laws and penalties

b. Impartial judges and fair trial to establish justice

We can see that each sphere of society has its own God-ordained purpose and responsibilities. What is granted to one must not be usurped by another. As pastors, we must understand that the church must not assume the role of the individual, family, or state. However, we must **also** recognize the church's broad role to instruct and support every sphere of life with biblical truth. Pastors should make sure their churches' teachings are covering all these spheres.

> ## Why do pastors often not teach biblical principles for society and government?

We have mentioned some pastors' concerns for revival and the role of prayer. Some pastors raise other issues in response to discussion about preaching political principles. Some say...[11]

"Christ crucified is the proper theme of ministers' discussion."

Ministers are to "preach Jesus Christ and him crucified" (1 Cor. 2:2), yes. But this does not exclude from the pulpit the duties of civil life. We are to preach "the whole counsel of God" (Acts 20:27), including both religious and civil duty. "Love the brotherhood of believers, fear God, honor the king" (1 Pet. 2:17).

"God's kingdom is not of this world."

God's kingdom is not *of* this world (Jn. 18:33, 36), but *over* this world. "The Lord has established his throne in heaven, and his kingdom rules over all" (Ps. 103:19). Though referred to as "the god of this world," we should never recognize as valid Satan's claim to sovereignty over the nations. Jesus is king over all.

"Ministers are to care for souls."

True. But, in order to promote the good of souls and not diminish spiritual-mindedness, one should include in his ministry a spiritual view of political movements. "So whether you eat or drink or whatever you do, do it all for the glory of God" (1 Cor. 10:31). Christianity is far more than a matter of the emotional or mental comfort of an individual. Christianity goes beyond that, to an individual's moral improvement and usefulness as a member of society. Such usefulness includes one's civil duties in which there is application of God's word to civil government.

"Christians are divided in political opinions."

Yes, and Christians are divided in religious opinions, too. But differences in opinion should not hinder the teaching of religious and civil duty. Pastors are not to preach opinions, but principles. Nor are pastors obligated to address every political issue. Rather, their role is distinguished by teaching biblical principles from which Christians can reason and arrive at their own conclusions.

"The early Christians were not involved with politics."

Paul and Peter, like Jesus, taught the believer's duty to civil government (Rom. 13; 1 Pet. 2:13-17). Paul was a champion of civil liberty, repeatedly protesting the violation of his civil rights (Acts 16:35, 39; Acts 22:22-29; Acts 24-26). We mentioned how Erastus was a fellow-minister of the gospel with Paul (Acts 19:22) who became involved in politics by serving as a commissioner of public works in Greece (Rom. 16:23).

"The Bible is only concerned about salvation."

The Bible is concerned very much about salvation. But it is also concerned with family issues (e.g., Eph. 6:1-4), economic issues (e.g., Deut. 23:19-20), civil issues (e.g., 1 Sam. 8), education issues (e.g., Deut. 6:4-9), environmental issues (e.g., Deut. 20:19-20), and much more.

"You cannot legislate morality."

While it is true that laws do not change people's hearts, it is a myth to suggest that legislation is not based on morality. There is no such thing as morally neutral legislation. The real question is, what is the basis of your moral standard – God or man? The minister has the duty of speaking forth the morality of God's word.

"Jesus was not a social reformer."

Jesus' earthly mission was to seek and save the lost, not to hold public office. However, Jesus clearly taught many principles for social reform, all of which he expects his ministers to teach today. That Jesus' teaching has radically reformed society is evident in its influence on all of Western civilization.

"The church should not be involved in social issues."

The characters and authors of the Bible, including Jesus Himself, involved themselves in social issues (slavery, the needs of the poor, politics, etc.). If these ministers of old did not consider it improper to discuss such issues, why should any minister today think it improper?

"Religion and politics do not mix."

It is the role of religion to inform politics (1 Tim. 3:15). The Old Testament prophets, John the Baptist, Jesus, Paul, Peter, and the entire Bible relate religion and politics in their teaching.

"There is a separation between church and state."

The Bible teaches that the church and state have separate jurisdictions. However, it also teaches that both are under the authority of God and His word and should operate in accordance with His principles.

"We're living in the last days."

Regardless of one's eschatological perspective, we all have religious and civil duties. In reference to the relationship of one's duties and the last days, Jesus told us "till I come, occupy" (Lk. 19:13). This means we must fulfill all the duties given us in Scripture whether we think he is coming back today or a thousand years from now.

"Aren't you advocating the Social Gospel?"

This refers to a movement in church history which emphasized the social dimensions of Christianity at the expense of emphasizing personal conversion. We must preach "the whole counsel of God," not just one dimension of it. This movement also became detached from distinctly biblical solutions to social issues. We are not advocating a social gospel in this book, but a gospel that affects all of life, from the individual to society.

"I'm afraid of Christian Reconstruction."

If Christian Reconstruction is equated with seizing government authority to impose all of the Mosaic civil code upon society, it is to be avoided. But, some who criticize Christian Reconstructionists do so without ever reading their materials. Reconstructionist materials often make clear the priority of revival and evangelism and a bottom-up influence in politics. In addition, sorting out the theological question of the continuity or discontinuity of the Mosaic civil code between the Old and New Testaments is a difficult issue, one which all streams of Christian faith need to better resolve. The attempt of Christian Reconstructionists to relate God's law to all of life is commendable.

"I don't want to be aligned with the Religious Right."

Christian involvement in politics should come out of an attitude of service. Servant leadership goes beyond asking "what can we get?" to "what can we give?" At the same time, it should not be merely a superficial or temporary involvement, nor only an issue-related involvement. In addition, though political party involvement is important, the kingdom of God must never be simply aligned with one political party. We should not be led so much by "conservative" or "liberal," or "right" or "left" agendas, but rather by the teachings of the Bible.

"I'm concerned about Dominion theology or 'Kingdom Now' teachings."

Often, Dominion theology or the "Kingdom Now" movement is equated with using political means to bring about salvation or the kingdom of God. Salvation and the kingdom of God are established by the atoning death and resurrection of Jesus Christ. Faithful Christian service in civil matters is our duty, but not our salvation. Furthermore, it must be recognized that the kingdom of God will not find total fulfillment until the end of the age.

It is understandable why pastors have concerns about preaching political principles from the pulpit. **But pastors must not let controversy scare them away from duty.** Pastors should take an active role in making sure that their parishioners are grounded in sound teaching and not false teaching. It is impossible to do this simply by not addressing political issues.

The more silence from the pulpit, the more problematic these things become. In fact, the pastor has the duty to actively teach the same biblical principles for government that Jesus and Paul taught.

> ## Are there other reasons pastors don't preach political principles from the pulpit?

In addition to theological misgivings and concerns about past efforts at reform, some pastors do not teach about civil duties for personal reasons.

1. They do not see it as a duty.

Some pastors are inclined to agree that the Bible teaches us about politics and society, but they view the pastor's role in teaching these things as only a privilege, not a duty. They might say, "That's fine for you. You seem to really have an understanding, enthusiasm, and calling to teach these things." While it is true that God seems to emphasize certain things in each individual's ministry, the Bible calls every pastor to a minimum standard of teaching all things that Jesus commanded, including civil duties as well as religious. **Every pastor has the duty, not just the privilege, to preach political principles from the pulpit.**

2. They have not been adequately trained.

Another reason pastors do not preach political principles is because they are not trained in most seminaries to do so. **Ministerial training today does very little, if anything, to equip ministers with a biblical understanding of government, law, economics, and education. Nor does it equip them with the ability to effectively articulate a biblical view**

of government and society and defend it against hostile world views. Our training seems to fall short both in content and methodology.

3. *They are not allowed time and opportunity.*

We can surely sympathize with the tremendous time, work, and stress loads placed on pastors today. Expectations are so high! They are to be preachers, counselors, managers, theologians, administrators, public relations directors, social coordinators, ceremonial officials, and on and on. It is therefore understandable when pastors respond to a call to study and preach political principles by saying, "I just don't have the time and opportunity to do this!" It appears that the congregational expectations of pastors has exceeded the biblical expectation of pastors. Their priority is to be given to prayer and the ministry of the word (Acts 6:4), and their goal is to equip the saints so that they will do the work of ministry (Eph. 4:12). **Expectations, structures, and models for pastoral ministry need to be re-examined and modified in light of Scripture. Doing so will free pastors to do what they are really called to do and what God requires of them.**

So, to conclude, we recall the first two questions we have raised. First, "What are pastors doing?" According to research, pastors are perceived by most as irrelevant. Second, "What should pastors be doing?" It appears that we need to recover the totality of our duties, the full use of the Bible, and the comprehensive mission to which we are called. This involves moving beyond revival and evangelism, to discipleship — including even the political, social, and cultural teachings of the Bible. To assist in this endeavor we ask: **"What have pastors done?"**

Chapter 4

The Clergy and the Founding of America

Pastors have not always been largely removed from influence in matters of government and society. This was especially true at the time of the founding of our nation.

> *Did the early American ministers teach biblical principles for government and society?*

There is no question that the clergy of early America preached political principles from the pulpit. In fact, so great was their role that historian John Wingate Thornton wrote in *The Pulpit of the American Revolution,* "...it is manifest, in the spirit of our history, in our annals, and by the general voice of the fathers of the republic, that, in a very great degree, — to the pulpit, the Puritan pulpit, we owe the moral force which won our independence."[13] The evidence for this is overwhelming. **For over a hundred years before the writing of the Declaration of Independence and our Constitution, all of the basic political principles found in them — those principles that have given us a degree of liberty and political stability**

greater than that of any other nation in history — were preached widely by the American ministers. In *The New England Clergy and the American Revolution,* historian Alice M. Baldwin documents the political preaching of early American ministers. From her book, we have compiled a list of political principles expounded in sermons and the names of their preachers as just a small sampling of the content of thousands of political sermons delivered in early America:[13]

Political Principles in Colonial Sermons

Principle	Pastor	Year
• the law of God is over all	Rev. Timothy Cutler	1717
• the law of nature and of nature's God	Rev. John Davenport	1669
• the purpose of government is the good of the people	Rev. John Bulkley	1713
• government is limited by law	Rev. Gershom Bulkley	1692
• consent of the governed	Rev. John Barnard	1738
• two spheres of liberty (civil and religious)	Rev. Benjamin Stevens	1761
• government is ordained of God	Rev. Ebenezer Pemberton	1710
• government is founded on compact or covenant	Rev. John Cotton	1645
• representative government	Rev. John Wise	1717
• duties of civil rulers	Rev. Jonathan Mayhew	1754
• right to resist tyranny	Rev. Nathaniel Appleton	1742
• mutual serviceableness of religion and civil government	Rev. Solomon Williams	1741
• civil disobedience	Rev. Jared Eliot	1738
• religious liberty and freedom of conscience	Rev. Elisha Williams	1744
• just war in self-defense	Rev. Jonas Clarke	1768
• opposition to slavery	Rev. Samuel Cooke	1770
• necessity of union	Rev. Robert Ross	1775
• written constitution	Rev. Jonas Clarke	1778
• natural, equal rights of life, liberty, and property	Rev. Samuel Langdon	1759

Early American ministers clearly understood that preaching political principles was a pastor's duty. Recognizing that the Bible speaks of not only religious duties but civil ones, they felt that to determine the nature and meaning of divine law and its application to civil government, and to make this clear to the people, was one of the chief aims of the clergy.[14] They carefully searched the Scriptures in order to provide biblical answers to the political questions of their day. Of their political preaching, Alice Baldwin writes, "They believed it their peculiar business to be 'watchmen on the tower,' to scent out and warn against danger and to set men right as to the principles upon which they were to act and the views they were to hold."[15]

Holding such convictions about their duty as ministers, **these pastors used a variety of vehicles through which to do their political preaching: occasional Sunday morning services; public days of fasting, prayer, and thanksgiving; weekly lectures on popular topics; election day sermons to magistrates; artillery sermons; letters and articles in newspapers; correspondence with friends; pamphlet literature; local government participation; and teaching in the colleges.**

The effect of their political preaching was remarkable. As Baldwin notes, the election sermons were particularly influential:

> *[F]or a hundred years before the Revolution and year by year throughout the long conflict, these sermons dealt with matters of government. They were heard by large audiences of clergy and laymen; they had the prestige of well-known names and of the colonial assembly attached to them; they were sent to friends in other colonies and in England and*

were distributed regularly to the country towns where they became, as Winsor styles them, "text-books of politics."[16]

This should not be taken to mean that only an elite few made an impact on the people with political preaching. To the contrary, these principles were so commonly preached in all the towns and countryside by nearly all the clergy that their repetition through so many years made them an integral part of the world-view of early Americans.[17] For example, so well versed was the typical church-goer in Scriptural political principles, that when colonial Americans were confronted with taxation without representation, "Every villager who attended church on the Sabbath day could talk learnedly of the reasons for refusing to pay the tax."[18] Thus, Alice Baldwin concludes, **it is clear "...that the New England clergy preserved, extended, and popularized the essential doctrines of political philosophy, thus making [them] familiar to every church-going New Englander."**[19]

Without a doubt, the early American ministers powerfully educated and influenced the masses with biblical political teaching. A study published in The *American Political Science Review* in 1984 confirmed this by showing that **the source most often cited by the founding fathers for their political ideas was the Bible, which accounted for 34 percent of all citations.**[20] In order to understand the impact of political preaching in early America, we can compare it to the power of the media today. **The typical colonial American adult listened to about 15,000 hours of biblical exposition by the clergy in his lifetime.**[21]

Were they relevant to the needs of their society?

These ministers exercised great influence and power in their society and were the most educated in their communities. **They extended biblical principles to every area of life:**[22]

- They colonized and formed our states (e.g., Connecticut by Rev. Thomas Hooker, Rhode Island by Rev. Roger Williams, and Pennsylvania by Quaker minister William Penn).

- They wrote our constitutions and laws (e.g., *The Fundamental Orders of Connecticut* by Rev. Thomas Hooker and *The Massachusetts Body of Liberties* by Rev. Nathaniel Ward).

- They established and defended civil liberties for the individual by serving as America's lawyers and judges up to the mid-1800's (e.g., Rev. Elisha Williams and Rev. Manassas Cutler).

- They established schools to perpetuate biblical principles of liberty (e.g., Boston Latin School by Rev. John Cotton).

- They established universities to perpetuate their own order — an influential clergy (e.g., Harvard by Rev. John Harvard and Yale by Congregational ministers).

John Witherspoon is just one example of the influential role of the clergy in early America. Rev. Witherspoon literally discipled the nation. He did so as a minister, President of the College of New Jersey (now Princeton), a signer of the Declaration of Independence, a member of over 100 committees in Congress, and a trainer of leaders of all types from his home in New Jersey. While serving as President of the College of New Jersey, Witherspoon discipled the following government officials over the years:[23]

- 1 President (James Madison)
- 1 Vice-President
- 3 Supreme Court Justices
- 10 Cabinet Members
- 12 Governors
- 60 Congressmen (21 Senators and 39 Congressmen)
- Plus many members of the Constitutional Convention and many state Congressmen

It is true that Witherspoon's achievements were extraordinary. However, it is also true that the clergy generally —ministers from the smallest village to the most prominent cities — provided an influential ministry relevant to the needs of their society. They provided leadership for their communities in the areas of religion, government, law, education, military affairs, economics, science, and medicine.[24] They were godly, pious men whose love for God would not allow them to lie aloof from their parishioners and communities, nor from the pressing needs of the same. They were not a class apart from society. Rather, they were the fellow-students, teachers, and friends of professional and business men and the pastors and guides of the less learned farmers.

Did they have a sound theology?

As we have said, these clergy were some of the most learned in their society. Graduating from Harvard, Princeton, Yale, and other outstanding universities, they received a first-rate general and theological education.

Their theology was based on the orthodox, traditional teaching of the Reformation. Their ideas did not stem from radical new teachings, but from long-established beliefs articulated by such theologians as Augustine or Calvin. Above all, they were committed to the Holy Scriptures which served as the basis for all their learning and instruction. Most of them were associated with the Congregational, Presbyterian, Episcopal, Lutheran, Reformed, Baptist, Methodist, and Roman Catholic denominations.

Arising out of a basic understanding of God as both Creator and Redeemer and the comprehensive nature of the Christian mission and duty of the minister, **the theology of the early American ministers can be characterized as holistic.** They knew, as Luther had said, that if they preached every part of the Christian faith except the one point at which they were being most greatly challenged, they would not be faithful to preach the whole counsel of God.

How were the ministers trained?

Having great confidence in the Bible as the source of all truth, the greatest fear of the early Americans was an ignorant and unlearned clergy that could not expound the meaning of Scripture as it applies to all of life.[25] Thus, they endeavored to establish outstanding institutions of learning to train their ministers. Of the 182 universities founded before the Civil War, all but 21 were established by Christian denominations for the purpose of training Christian ministers and leaders.[26]

We know that these ministers exhibited a tremendous ability and influence in their society. **What was the food that made these giants? What kind of training equipped them for such exploits?** The training of early American ministers is noteworthy both for its content and its methodology. As for content, ministers were held to a very high standard in their ability to read and understand the Bible in its original languages (Greek, Hebrew, and Aramaic). For example, to earn a Bachelors Degree, one must be "found able to read the originale of the Old and New Testaments into the Latin tongue and to resolve them logically."[27] Their studies in theology were based on an understanding of both the Creation Commission and the Redemption Commission (as we call them) derived from the writings of William Ames, John Calvin, and others.

Ministers studied theology rigorously. But their divinity curriculum also required studying the biblical principles of logic, ethics, politics, rhetoric, history, and natural science.[28] It was only in the 19th century that there developed a cleavage between divinity and the other disciplines. This philosophical shift was implemented in part through the creation of separate Schools of Divinity in the leading universities during the early 1800's. Gradually, theology was no longer the "queen of the sciences" among the leading universities.

While the content of the early American ministers' training gave them a solid biblical understanding, their ability to articulate such an understanding on a great variety of topics is reflected in the titles of some of their disputations. Disputations were a regular part of each student's school week and amounted to debate-like exercises with fellow-students and faculty. They were designed to develop students' oratorical, logical, and theological skills. By training ministers to reason from principles of Scripture to every aspect of life, they were equipped to address the leading philosophical, political, and religious questions of the day in an informed and articulate manner. Here are some of the many disputation topics at Harvard in the 17th and 18th centuries on the subject of society and the state:[29]

- "Is a monarchical government the best?"

- "Is the voice of the people the voice of God?"

- "Does civil government originate from compact?"

- "Is it lawful to resist the supreme magistrate?"

- "Is civil government absolutely necessary?"

Was there a common core of belief across the denominations?

Early American ministers seem to have been fairly unified in terms of their basic convictions about preaching political principles from the pulpit. Baldwin points out that both Calvinist and Arminian believed in a divine law and fundamental constitution which was binding upon God and man.[30] Many historians note a common core of belief, a common mind of the Colonial Era which represented a biblical world view held by clergy and laity alike. **Nearly all ministers accepted as their duty the preaching of political and other relevant doctrines, regardless of denominational or doctrinal affiliation.**

Do the American clergymen of the past serve as worthy models for today?

It is important that we do not look back in history and idealize the early American clergy. They had weaknesses as well as strengths, and they also had circumstances different in many ways from ours today. Nevertheless, we can see from what has been discussed in previous paragraphs that the early American clergy have given us many positive examples of effective, biblical ministry. These positive examples include: a learned clergy; a holistic, relevant theology; a commitment to preach the whole counsel of God; reliance on the Bible as the source of all truth; ability to articulate biblical principles to all of life; influential involvement in their communities and the affairs of the day; effectively training their ministers; preaching biblical principles for government and society; emphasizing godly character; and maintaining unity across denominational lines for the purpose of furthering God's kingdom.

What was the fruit of the colonial clergy's involvement?

We can assess the quality and value of the colonial clergy's involvement by the fruit it produced in our nation. By establishing the religious and political underpinnings of America, they can be credited with helping to establish the most free and prosperous nation in history. What other nation has experienced the liberty, justice, wealth, and security our nation has enjoyed? Our nation is testimony to the blessings of God on those who faithfully proclaim his whole word.

Chapter 5

What Pastors and the Church Can Do Now

So far, we have observed a lack of preaching and teaching on principles of government and society among today's pastors. We have received encouragement to recover this aspect of our ministries through the example of past American pastors. The question now remains: what course of action should pastors and the church take both now and in the future?

What have pastors and Christian leaders said?

John Wycliffe said of his English Bible:

This Bible is for the government of the people, by the people, and for the people. [31]

Martin Luther said:

If I profess with the loudest voice and clearest exposition every portion of the truth of God except precisely that little point which the world and the devil are at that moment attacking, I am not confessing Christ, however boldly I may be professing Christ. [32]

John Calvin wrote:

Civil authority is, in the sight of God, not only sacred and lawful, but the most sacred, and by far the most honorable, of all stations in mortal life.

Colonial clergyman Jonathan Mayhew stated in his *Discourse Concerning Unlimited Submission:*

Although there be a sense... in which Christ's kingdom is not of this world, his inspired apostles have, nevertheless, laid down some general principles concerning the office of civil rulers and the duty of subjects... It is the duty of all Christian people to inform themselves what it is which their religion teaches concerning that subjection which they owe to the higher powers.[33]

John Jay was one of the authors of the *Federalist Papers* and the first Chief Justice of the Supreme Court. He also served as the President of the the American Bible Society. He said:

Providence has given to our people the choice of their rulers, and it is the duty, as well as the privilege and interest, of our Christian nation to select and prefer Christians for their rulers.[34]

The American preacher of the nineteenth century, Charles Finney, wrote in his *Revivals of Religion* that one of the things that must be done to assure the continuance of revival was this:

"The Church must take right ground in regard to politics.... The time has come that Christians must vote for honest men, and take consistent ground in politics, or the Lord will curse them.... God cannot sustain this free and blessed country, which we love and pray for, unless the Church will take right ground. Politics are a part of a religion in such a

country as this, and Christians must do their duty to the country as a part of their duty to God.... He [God] will bless or curse this nation, according to the course they [Christians] take [in politics]. "35

Charles Hodge wrote:

If Christ is really King, exercising original and immediate jurisdiction over the State as really as He does over the church, it follows necessarily that the general denial or neglect of his rightful lordship, any prevalent refusal to obey that Bible which is the open law-book of his kingdom, must be followed by political and social as well as moral and religious ruin. If professing Christians are unfaithful to the authority of their Lord in their capacity as citizens of the State, they cannot expect to be blessed by the indwelling of the Holy Ghost in their capacity as members of the Church. The kingdom of Christ is one, and cannot be divided in life or in death. If the Church languishes, the State cannot be in health; and if the State rebels against its Lord and King, the Church cannot enjoy his favour. If the Holy Ghost is withdrawn from the Church, he is not present in the State; and if he, the only "Lord, the Giver of life," be absent, then all order is impossible, and the elements of society lapse backward to primeval night and chaos. 36

Is this a matter of privilege or duty?

You may say, "This preaching political principles from the pulpit seems to be basically legitimate in light of Scripture and history. But that's not *my* calling." When ministers' vigorous and influential involvement in matters of society and government declined rapidly after the 18th century, Rev. Alexander McLeod, in 1815, was pressed to give a defense of ministers preaching political principles from the pulpit. After delivering an able defense, he made the point that not only was it the *privilege* of every pastor to preach political principles, but it was his *duty*. He said,

> *I claim the privilege of explaining the law of my God. I claim it, too, not merely as a privilege, which I am at liberty to use. It is not even optional to the ministers of religion whether to use it or not: they are bound by their public instructions, as ambassadors for Christ, to raise a voice which shall reach to both the cottage and the throne, and teach their several occupants their respective duties. "Go," said our arisen Lord to his ministers, when handing to them their commission, "disciple all nations, teaching them to observe all things whatsoever I have commanded you." We must, my brethren, in order to be faithful to our exalted employer, have it in our power to say upon a review of our ministry, after an example of approved excellence, "I have not shunned to declare unto you the whole counsel of God."[37]*

What is your response to all this?

In the light of Scripture and history, we have considered three questions in this booklet with respect to the role of the pastor in preaching biblical principles for government and society. First, we asked, **"What are pastors doing?"** We concluded that the church today is perceived by most as irrelevant to the way we live. This has been a source of frustration for many pastors laboring in their churches. However, we believe we pastors can capture a vibrant, biblical, relevant ministry by:

- Accepting our duty to teach **all** of Scripture

- Setting as our goal the comprehensive Christian mission

- Teaching Jesus' and the Bible's teaching about society and government

- Applying the principles of biblical jurisdiction – the distinct roles of the individual, the family, the church, and the state

- Endeavoring to bring about the reformation of society as well as revival

- Advocating both prayer **and** action in our efforts to impact society

- Overcoming theological, philosophical, and personal stumbling blocks to fulfilling our pastoral duties related to the civil as well as religious teachings of the Bible

- Training our ministers to effectively articulate biblical principles for all of life

- Structuring our churches and ministries in order to provide the time and freedom pastors need to teach biblical principles for society and government

We asked, **"What have pastors done?"** We concluded that the early American ministers **did** preach political principles from the pulpit. In fact, it is clear that they:

- Perceived preaching political principles as their duty

- Used many vehicles in order to preach political principles

- Were extremely influential in society

- Were relevant to the needs of their parishioners and communities

- Had a sound, orthodox theology

- Effectively trained ministers for biblical, academic, spiritual, and practical excellence

- Held a common core of beliefs across denominations, a biblical world view, which enabled them to unite for the furthering of God's kingdom

- Served in many ways as positive examples for pastors today

We have also asked, **"What should pastors do?"** We urge you to accept the theological and historical observations presented in this booklet in favor of ministers preaching political principles from the pulpit. But, we also challenge you to accept this on the personal level, to accept it not merely as your privilege, but as your duty.

It is our hope that this booklet reflects some of God's will for pastors as expressed in Scripture. Based on that hope, we challenge pastors today to do two things. **First, every pastor should teach biblical principles for government and society.** He must proclaim the truth and equip and organize his flock to obey it. **Second,** as an example to the flock (1 Pet. 5:3), **every pastor should model faithfulness to the civil and social duties given to Christians in Scripture.** His personal example will display integrity, give credibility to his message, and do a lot to motivate his congregation to faithfulness.

This is a tall order. It will take time to phase this teaching and modeling into the life of a church, so it is best to take one step at a time. Perhaps a first priority, after beginning to equip others, is to focus on choosing government representatives. This is surely one of the most basic and important Christian civil duties.

THE PASTOR EQUIPS THE SAINTS...

As pastor, you can equip the saints by:

- **Preaching sermons:**
    Use holidays, election days, historic dates, crisis events
- **Teaching classes:**
    Include classes on government, society, and culture in your curriculum
- **Establishing a resource center in your church:**
    Include books, newsletters, journals, articles, papers, teaching materials, videos, organization lists, and any other practical, user-friendly, relevant, and useful tools; many are available
- **Identifying members who are leaders in different spheres of civil and social action and encouraging and discipling them**
- **Initiating small groups for equipping members for ministry:**
    Groups could be organized vocationally (e.g., lawyers, educators, businessmen) or topically (e.g., government, education, economics)
- **Modeling obedience to civil and social duties:**
    Voting, awareness of issues, benevolence, involvement in the community, etc.

...FOR WORKS OF SERVICE.

Church members will then be equipped to bring reform in all areas:

- **Individuals:**
  In the areas of spiritual maturity, edification ministries, and work
- **Family:**
  In the areas of sanctity of life, rearing children, education, health, welfare, and finances
- **Church:**
  In the areas of biblical truth, corporate worship, sacraments, church discipline, and discipling, equipping, and organizing believers for various works of service
- **State:**
  In the areas of protecting law-abiding citizens, punishing criminals, police force, protection of rights from abuses, election of representatives, just laws, impartial judges, and fair trials

Shortly before John Witherspoon signed the Declaration of Independence in 1776, the Congress appointed a General Fast Day for the colonies. In observance of the day of fasting and prayer, Witherspoon preached a sermon at the College of New Jersey (Princeton), entitled *The Dominion of Providence Over the Affairs of Men*. Typical of clergy of the time, he included "some exhortations to duty" and proclaimed that "your duty to God, to your country, to your families, and to yourselves is the same." Witherspoon conveyed the theological perspective that once was dominant in American churches—that duties to God and family are no more important or sacred than one's duty to the civil arena. They are the same in Scripture. In other words, they are equally binding upon the believer. Every

Christian will give account for his civil responsibilities as he will for his individual, parental, and spiritual duties.

The enumeration of the duties of the believer by Witherspoon reflects the historical understanding of the essential elements of Christian discipleship and pastoral teaching to which clergy from the Protestant Reformation up through the American Revolution were faithful. They follow along the lines of the three Divinely ordained institutions in Scripture—Family, Church and State—plus the duties of the individual (listed earlier, see pages 28-31). They also correspond to the four Biblical commandments enjoining love, as found in Luke 10:27, Ephesians 5:25-29, and Titus 2:4. The following chart shows this relationship.

Witherspoon's Duties	Nature	Institution	Commandment
"To God"	Spiritual	Church	Love God
"To Country"	Civil/Social	State	Love Neighbor
"To Family"	Marital/Parental	Family	Love spouse/kids
"To Yourself"	Individual	—	Love Self

As you seek to disciple and equip the saints for works of service, it is vital to include all the duties God has set forth in His Word. If we neglect any of them, the low view that many have of the church today will continue, and our nation will move further away from godliness and more into bondage.

Cynicism, pessimism, and dissatisfaction are widespread today with respect to the church and the state. But there is hope. The gospel, in all its fullness and with all its accompanying doctrines, proclaimed by men of God, has the power to transform both individuals and nations. By serving as **watchmen on the walls**, we can fulfill our pastoral duties and see the power of God transform our cities and nation. This has happened before; it can happen again.

END NOTES

[1] George Barna, *What Americans Believe: An Annual Survey of Values and Religious Views in the United States* (Ventura, CA: Regal Books, 1991), p. 184.

[2] Ibid.

[3] George Barna and William Paul McKay, *Vital Signs: Emerging Social Trends and the Future of American Christianity* (Westchester, IL: Crossway Books, 1984), p. 2.

[4] Ibid., p. 4.

[5] George Barna, *User Friendly Churches* (Ventura, CA: Regal Books, 1991), p. 73.

[6] As quoted in Gary DeMar, *You've Heard It Said: 15 Biblical Misconceptions That Render Christians Powerless* (Brentwood, TN: Woglemuth & Hyatt, Publishers, Inc., 1991), p. 23.

[7] Kenneth Gentry, The Greatness of the Great Commission, Tyler, TX: Institute for Christian Economics, 1990, p. 75.

[8] Stephen K. McDowell and Mark A. Beliles, *Liberating the Nations*, (Charlottesville, VA: Providence Foundation, 1993), pp. 141-154.

[9] McDowell and Beliles, pp. 77-88

[10] Ibid., pp. 89-92.

[11] Adapted from DeMar and Alexander McLeod, *A Scriptural View of the Character, Causes, and Ends of the Present War*, (New York: Eastburn, Kirk and Co.; Whiting and Watson; and Smith and Forman, 1815).

[12] John Wingate Thornton, *The Pulpit of the American Revolution* (Boston: Gould and Lincoln, 1860), p. XXXVII.

[13] Alice M. Baldwin, *The New England Clergy and the American Revolution* (New York: Ungar Publishing Co., 1928), pp. 13, 15, 16, 18, 20, 22, 25, 28, 35, 37, 38, 43, 49, 65, 107, 128, 133, 138.

[14] Ibid., p. 13.

[15] Ibid., p. 33.

[16] Ibid., p. 6.

[17] Ibid., p. 6.

[18] Ibid., p. 104.

[19] Ibid., p. xii.

[20]Donald S. Lutz, "The Relative Influence of European Writers on Late Eighteenth-Century American Political Thought," *American Political Science Review* 189 (1984): 189-97.

[21]Beliles and McDowell, *America's Providential History*, p. 122.

[22]Ibid., (see Chapters 6-11).

[23]Norman V. Pope, "Educator, Minister, Patriot," *Nation Under God* (Great Neck, NY: Channel Press, 1957), pp. 41-42.

[24]Baldwin, p. 169.

[25]Nathanial Appleton as quoted in Rosalie J. Slater, *Teaching and* Learning America's Christian History (San Francisco, CA: Foundation for American Christian Education, 1980), pp. 38-39.

[26]Donald G. Tewksbury, *The Founding of American Colleges and Universities Before the Civil War* (New York: Arno Press and the New York Times, 1952, 1969), pp. 55-56.

[27]E. G. Dexter "Appendix C: The First Rules for the Government of the Students of Harvard University, Printed in 1642," *History of Education in the U. S.* (New York: The Macmillan Co., 1904), p. 592.

[28]Colyer Meriwether, *Our Colonial Curriculum, 1607-1776* (Washington, D. C.: Capital Publishing Co., 1907), p. 52.

[29]Meriwether, p. 249.

[30]Baldwin, p. 18.

[31]Verna M. Hall and Rosalie J. Slater, *The Bible and the Constitution of the United States of America* (San Francisco: Foundation for American Christian Education, 1983), p. 14.

[32] Gary DeMar, *God and Government, A Biblical and Historical Study* (Atlanta: American Vision Press, 1982), p. viii.

[33]Beliles and McDowell, *America's Providential History*, p. 118.

[34]Ibid., p. 264.

[35] Ibid., p. 267.

[36]Demar, p. ix.

[37] McLeod, p. 28.

BIBLIOGRAPHY

Ames, William. *The Marrow of Theology*. Boston: Pilgrim Press, 1968.

Bailyn, Bernard. *Education in the Forming of American Society*. Chapel Hill, NC: The University of North Carolina Press, 1960.

Bainton, Roland H. *Yale and the Ministry: A History of Education for the Christian Ministry at Yale from the Founding in 1701*. New York: Harper and Brothers, 1957.

Baldwin, Alice Mary. *The New England Clergy and the American Revolution*. New York: F. Ungar Pub. Co., 1965.

Barna, George. *What Americans Believe: An Annual Survey of Values and Religious Views in the United States*. Ventura, CA: Regal Books, 1991.

Barron, Bruce. *Heaven On Earth?: The Social and Political Agendas of Dominion Theology*. Grand Rapids: Zondervan,1992.

Beliles, Mark A. and Stephen K. McDowell. *America's Providential History*. Charlottesville, VA: Povidence Press, 1989.

Beliles, Mark. *The Missing Keys for the Total Reformation of America*. Charlottesville, VA: Providence Foundation, 1988.

Cole, Franklin. *They Preached Liberty: An Anthology of Timely Quotations from New England Ministers of the American Revolution on the Subject of Liberty, Its Source, Nature, Obligations, Types, and Blessings*. Indianapolis: Liberty Press, 1977.

Collins, Varsum Lansing. *President Witherspoon*. New York: Arno Press and The New York Times, 1969.

Colson, Charles. *The Role of the Church in Society*. Wheaton, IL: Victor Books, 1986.

Cornelison, Isaac A. *The Relation of Religion to Civil Government in the United States of America: A State Without A Church, But Not Without A Religion*. New York: Da Capo Press, 1970.

Cross, Arthur Lyon. *The Anglican Episcopate and the American Colonies*. Cambridge, MA: Harvard University Press, 1924, c1902.

Cushing, John D. *The Laws of the Pilgrims*. Pilgrim Society, 1977.

DeMar, Gary. *"You've Heard It Said": 15 Biblical Misconceptions That Render Christians Powerless*. Brentwood, TN: Woglemuth & Hyatt, Publishers, Inc., 1991.

Dexter, E. G. *History of Education in the United States*. New York: The Macmillan Co., 1904.

Eidsmoe, John. *Christianity and the Constitution: The Faith of Our Founding Fathers*. Grand Rapids, MI: Baker Book House, 1987.

Gambrell, Mary Latimer. *Ministerial Training in Eighteenth-Century New England*. New York: Columbia University Press, 1937.

Gentry, Kenneth L. *The Greatness of the Great Commission*. Tyler, TX: Institute for Christian Economics, 1990.

Goen, C. C. *Broken Churches, Broken Nation: Denominational Schisms and the Coming of the American Civil War*. Macon, GA: Mercer University Press, 1985.

Hall, Verna M., and Rosalie J. Slater. *The Bible and the Constitution of the United States of America*. San Francisco: Foundation for American Christian Education, 1983.

Headley, Joel Tyler. *The Chaplains and Clergy of the Revolution*. New York: C. Scribner, 1864.

Heimert, Alan. *Religion and the American Mind*. Cambridge, MA: Harvard University Press, 1966.

Hyneman, Charles S. and Donale S. Lutz. *American Political Writing During the Founding Era, 1760-1805*, Vols. I & II. Indianapolis: Liberty Press, 1983.

Loring, James Spear. *The Hundred Boston Orators Appointed by the Muncipal Authorities and Other Public Bodies, from 1770 to 1852*. Boston: Jewett, 1852.

Mather, Cotton. *Manductio Ad Ministerium: Directions for a Candidate of the Ministry*. New York: Columbia University Press, 1938.

McDowell, Stephen K. and Mark A. Beliles. *Liberating the Nations*. Charlottesville, VA: Providence Foundation, 1993.

McLeod, Alexander. *A Scriptural View of the Character, Causes, and Ends of the Present War*. New York: Eastburn, Kirk and Co.; Whiting and Watson; and Smith and Forman, 1815.

Mead, Sidney. "The Rise of the Evangelical Conception of the Ministry in America (1607-1850)" in H. Richard Niebuhr and Daniel D. Williams, eds., *The Ministry in Historical Perspectives*. New York: Harper & Brothers, 1956.

Meriwether, Colyer. *Our Colonial Curriculum*. Washington, D. C.: Capital Publishing Co., 1907.

Miller, Perry. *The New England Mind*. New York: The Macmillan Co., 1939.

Miller, Samuel. *Letters to Presbyterians On the Present Crisis in the Presbyterian Church*. Philadelphia: Anthony Finley, 1833.

Miller, Thomas, ed. *The Selected Writings of John Witherspoon*. Carbondale, IL: Southern Illinois University Press, 1990.

Reichley, A. James. *Religion in American Public Life*. Washington, D. C.: The Brookings Institution, 1985.

Rossiter, Clinton. *Seedtime of the Republic*. New York: Harcourt, Brace, and Co., 1953.

Rowe, H. Edward. *Save America!* Old Tappan, NJ: Fleming H. Revell Company, 1971.

Sandoz, Ellis, ed. *Political Sermons of the American Founding Era, 1730-1805*. Indianapolis: Liberty Press, 1991.

Stohlman, Martha Lou Lemmon. *John Witherspoon: Parson, Politician, Patriot*. Louisville, KY: Westminster/John Knox Press, 1976.

Stout, Harry S. *The New England Soul: Preaching and Religious Culture in Colonial New England*. New York: Oxford University Press, 1986.

Thornton, John Wingate. *The Pulpit of the American Revolution*. New York: Da Capo Press, reprint, 1860.

Van Tyne, Claude. *The Causes of the War of Independence*. New York: Peter Smith, 1951.

Whitehead, John. *An American Dream*. Westchester, IL: Crossway Books, 1987.

Wines, E. C. *The Hebrew Republic*. American Presbyterian Press, reprint, no date.

The Providence Foundation

The Providence Foundation is a Christian educational organization whose mission is to spread liberty, justice, and prosperity among the nations by educating individuals in a biblical worldview. We use historical examples of Christian statesmen and citizens who believed in "Divine Providence" and applied Scriptural principles to public affairs, and therefore significantly influenced their nations. Rather than being issues oriented, the Providence Foundation emphasizes a biblical and principled approach to reasoning and its application in families, schools, businesses, government, and politics.

Numerous Providence Foundation representatives and associates around the world work to fulfill the mission and goals. They especially assist churches in fulfilling their responsibility of teaching and equipping people to apply biblical principles in all of life. Our long-term goal is to restore to America's homes, churches, and schools the ideas that form the foundation of freedom and to infuse these same ideas into the fabric of all nations.

The Providence Foundation produces biblical worldview resources in many languages; offers numerous presentations, talks, seminars, and Christian history tours; trains people to instruct others; and encourages leaders to establish local educational and reformational groups. For information on scheduling a presentation or seminar, call our office at 804-978-4535.

About the Authors

Mark Beliles has served in the ministry for over 20 years and is presently the pastor of Grace Covenant Church in Charlottesville, Virginia. His concern for equipping pastors and Christians in applying biblical principles to all of life led him to help start the Providence Foundation in 1983. He now serves as Chairman of the Board of Directors. He has authored and co-authored several books, has participated in training many Christian leaders for the ministry, and has assisted in establishing churches in America and other nations. Mark and his wife, Nancy, have three children.

Stephen McDowell, President of the Providence Foundation, has taught inspiring seminars throughout the United States as well as in Asia, South America, Europe, Australia, and Africa. He has trained thousands of people from 70 countries, consulted with numerous government officials, assisted in writing political documents and starting political parties, and helped establish classes on godly reformation in numerous churches. He has authored and co-authored several books and videos. Stephen pastored churches for six years before moving to Charlottesville to help Mark start the Providence Foundation. He and his wife, Beth, have four children.

Bruce Anderson, a Pastor of Kempsville Presbyterian Church in Virginia Beach, Virginia, received a degree in Divinity and Public Policy from Regent University, writing his thesis on *Recovering the Clergy's Role in American Public Affairs*. Bruce interned with Mark and Stephen to produce *Watchmen on the Walls*. Bruce and Ellen have three children.

Providence Foundation Resources

Books

America's Providential History (B01) $16.95

How the Lord guided our nation from the very beginning. Proof from history: our nation grew from Christian principles. How to bring them back into the mainstream.

Liberating the Nations (B02) $13.95

God's plan, fundamental principles, essential foundations, and structures necessary to build Christian nations.

Defending the Declaration (B04) $13.95

How the Bible and Christianity influenced the writing of the Declaration.

Watchmen on the Walls (B06) $6.95

The role of pastors in equipping Christians to fulfill their civil duties.

In God We Trust (B03) $13.95

A Christian tour guide for historic sites in Washington D.C., Philadelphia, Jamestown, Williamsburg, Richmond, Mt. Vernon, Charlottesville, and more.

Thomas Jefferson's Abridgement (B05) $6.95

An abridgement of the Words of Jesus of Nazareth as compiled by Jefferson while President. With an introductory essay on Jefferson's religious beliefs.

In Search of Democracy (B07) $5.95

Foundations, framework, and historical development of biblical government and law.

Independence, Drums of War, vol. 1 (B08) $7.95
Bunker Hill, Drums of War, vol. 2 (B09) $7.95
A Captive in Williamsburg, Drums of War, vol. 3 (B10) $7.95

Drums of War is a series of historical novels for youth and young adults designed to teach in an enjoyable way the principles, events, and persons behind America's independence.

The Ten Commandments and Modern Society (B11) $4.95

Restoring America's Christian Education (B12) $4.95

A Guide to American Christian Education (B13) $39.95

Hardback book by Jim Rose examines the Principle Approach to Education, including Christian philosophy, methodology, notebooks, and various subjects.

Videos/Game

The Story of America's Liberty (VT01) $19.95

A 65-minute video that looks at the influence of Christianity in the beginning of America, examining principles and providential occurrences.

Dawn's Early Light (VT02) $19.95

A 28-minute version of *The Story of America's Liberty* with up-dated statistics.

America: the Game (GM1) $29.95

An exciting way to learn about the history of America and God's hand in it. Over 2000 questions.

dios

Search of Democracy Four-tape series on biblical government and law.	(ATS02)	$19.95
e Principle Approach to Education for Home r Church Schools A biblical approach to teaching the academic subjects. Includes 24 tapes and a 160-page manual.	(ATS01)	$109.95
erating the Nations: Developing a Biblical Vorldview Seven-tape series with outlines.	(ATS03)	$39.95
erica's Freedom: Founded on Faith	(AT15)	$4.95
Cross, No Crown: Exemplified in the Life of lliam Penn	(AT1)	$4.95
forming the Nations — an Example from the e of Noah Webster	(AT2)	$4.95
aching History from a Providential Perspective	(AT10)	$4.95
e Principle Approach	(AT9)	$4.95
inciple Approach: Teaching History & Literature	(AT19)	$4.95
d Governs in the Affairs of Men	(AT11)	$4.95
lical Economics	(AT7)	$4.95
nest Money and Banking	(AT8)	$4.95
lical Government and Law	(AT5)	$4.95
rming a Christian Union	(AT6)	$4.95
men: Preservers & Propagators of Liberty as achers of the Human Race	(AT13)	$4.95
ndamental Principles of Christian Nations	(AT3)	$4.95
rist's Teaching on Public Affairs	(AT4)	$4.95
blical Principles of Business, Exemplified by rus Hall McCormick	(AT16)	$4.95
e Hold These Truths — Governmental Principles America's Founders	(AT12)	$4.95
e American Christian Revolution — ristianity: Foundation of America's Liberty	(AT14)	$4.95
lucation and the Kingdom of God	(AT17)	$4.95
e Biblical Relationship of Church and State	(AT18)	$4.95
ophetic Christian Statesmanship	(AT20)	$4.95
e Ten Commandments & Modern Society	(AT21)	$4.95

RESPONSE & ORDER FORM

I want to join you in spreading God's liberty, justice, and prosperity among the na
and restoring to America's homes, churches, and schools the ideas that form the fo
dation of freedom by becoming a:

☐ **SPECIAL SUPPORTER**: those who contribute any amount toward the
ongoing ministry of the Providence Foundation receive the *Providential Perspective* and *Reformation Report*. Enclosed is my gift of: $

☐ **MEMBER**: those who contribute $100 or more per year receive our
newsletters, a 30% discount on all our books, videos, and materials,
plus discounts to our Summer Institute. I will send a regular gift of
$_____ per month / quarter / year (circle one). Enclosed is my gift of: $

I wish to order the following items from your catalog:

Quan.	Title/Product code	Price	Total

Shipping & Handling:	Subtotal	
* US Mail: $3.00 minimum, 10% if over $30. * UPS: $5.00 minimum, 12% if over $50.	Sales tax (VA orders add 4.5%)	
(Game orders will be sent UPS.)	**Shipping**	
	Member disct. (30%)	
Total contribution and order: $	**TOTAL**	

Method of Payment: ❑ Check/Money Order ❑ VISA ❑ Mastercard ❑ AmEx ❑

Credit Card No.:_____ Exp. date: _____

Signature:_____

SHIP TO:

Name:_____

Address:_____

City:_____State:_____Zip:_____

Phone:(_____)_____

Email:_____

Make checks payable to
Providence Foundat
PO Box 6759
Charlottesville, VA 22
Phone/Fax: 804-978-4

Also, order by phone or at w
www.providencefoundation